Women of the Word

Art and Story by
Mary Lou Sleevi

AVE MARIA PRESS NOTRE DAME, INDIANA 46556

About the author:

The 16 *Women of the Word* paintings that appear in this book grew out of Mary Lou Sleevi's own probing for meaning. After years of involvement in church life "it was not all that meaningful anymore...the old answers weren't good enough." She and a small group of women with like concerns wrestled with "the whole notion of personhood," and she became determined to use her artistic gifts to explore what the scriptures have to say to women.

Sleevi, who did commercial art while in college (Avila and Marquette) and while raising five children, studied under the late Ralph de Burgos. When her husband Gene began studying for his degree in Pastoral Counseling, Mary Lou began to paint her women of scripture.

The paintings have been exhibited widely throughout the Washington D.C. area—in galleries, churches, colleges, and at retreats and conferences. They have been exhibited at an annual meeting of the National Conference of Catholic Bishops, in the rotunda of the United Methodist Building on Capitol Hill, and have been featured in the nationally syndicated television program "Real to Reel."

Citations from THE NEW JERUSALEM BIBLE, copyright © 1985 by Darton, Longman & Todd, Ltd. and Doubleday & Company, Inc. Used by permission of the publisher.

Library of Congress Catalog Card Number: 89-83992

International Standard Book Number: 0-87793-404-5

Cover and text design: Katherine Robinson Coleman

Printed and bound in the United States of America.

Contents

Foreword

God is The Artist.

God paints all day, every day, every moment.
God has imagination and time.
God loves the palette
because color is light
and God is Light.
Each new day adds its measure
to the sum total of light
in time.

Dayspring
supplies great quantities of colors.
Never tiring,
The Artist applies layers of paint
on each work projected.
The Imager does likenesses.
Even in the rough,
there is something of God in each of us,
and something of each of us in God.

The Original, who does only originals,
never paints by numbers.
Ever since Eden,
no two beings nor moments
are ever the same.

Woman's creation
was handled with more ingenuity than man's,
but each was an "I" before "they" were a "we."
Each is The Artist's "ecstatic moment."
And God's moments carry.

The Maker of heavenly order
with the universe in hand,
chose a planet for The Studio,
a messy workplace not set in a garden.

Beauty and Truth emanated as light of the world
from a carpenter's shop
in Jesus.
His Spirit emerges anywhere anytime
to renew the face of the earth
on its people.

To breathe us creative again and again.
With that kind of Breath,
we are all apprenticed artists.
From the beginning,
the mist of the Spirit may have been sweat:
Holy Sweat, but sweat nonetheless.
Working artists find that the message conveys.

Hands mix paint, over and over,
knowing that hardly any color
that's right for a canvas
comes right from a tube.

They discover the purple in orange,
and the orange in purple.
Eyes denote and develop "negative spaces"
that work on an artist
as part of the art,
if an artist works on them.

To image The Artist is to have paint on one's hands —
from morning on.
To share the workplace
where darkness is lived every day.
Where light fades by the moment,
where color goes dull,
where it's mostly a mix.
And where nothing, really, will ever be neat.

To believe in The Artist
is to be a canvas unfinished,
to be a space
where the First One is free.
And to discover the brush in my hand
is only The Artist believing in me.

God spoke "Be not afraid,"
as an artist to artists.

9

To let God be the artist in me
is to let something happen —
upsetting the order I've pre-arranged,
splashing it away with red paint.
To indulge the very mess:
to play with it and let it play with me.
To get angry.
To begin again . . .
and again and again and again
as God does;
till I, too, make something new.
And am glad.

Introduction

The paintings in my collection of *Women of the Word* have been up and down many times in ecumenical movement from wall to wall. They have been sung to and danced to and watched with and prayed with, among all kinds of people, women and men.

Settings varied: there was space to be quiet.

At one presentation, a woman from each continent, in the dress of her culture, spoke of her own experiences in relation to a painting. All were sisters of Wisdom: On their faces was profound revelation!

The paintings depict some of the women and some of the moments at the heart of the gospel and salvation story. Within the context of biblical events, imagination is free. I express each woman in an encounter with God, the moment which I felt was a liberating experience. Each, I believe, is breaking Good News.

I focus on faces and hands, since good news shows on a face or a body: and so much that is caring — like the making of art — is done by a hand. Each canvas began and ended as a painting.

Then I added the reflections. Developed from the paintings, they speak of the person, set the moment, expand meaning for me, within her larger story. They are the fruit of prayerful thought, enriched immeasurably by the sharing of many people.

This book is another coming together. I hope viewers and readers will add to its content.

———————————

There is great religious art that has left bad impressions, and bad art has been called good because it is pious.

Art communicates something of Mystery: If this is message art, so be it!

Painting with acrylics, I use a very disciplined, contemporary art form, hard edge. I freely adapt, keeping a feel for the abstract. Elongation is employed for emphasis in design.

Hard edge is flat and precise. It *makes* simple. Stripping to essentials, it allows nothing fuzzy. It opens to interpretation. Each space, shape and color stands on its own and in relationship — even negative space.

Hard edge makes choices every inch of the way. Its way is a process: a converging and a purging. To me, hard edge somehow discloses that whatever doesn't work aesthetically is simply extraneous.

———————————

A canvas was primed, the gesso was dry. Mary of Magdala was first. I stood, then sat, at an easel and felt chaos and void, grays and umbers. Maybe there's something of the Spirit just in brooding over it. When a painter prays, "Let there be light," nothing seems to happen.

Because an artist shows up in the painting, I looked back at blank canvas for a long time, looking for a face amid shadows, rocks and clutter. But the face Mary looked for was *his*. I found her inside me, just seeing Jesus. It was that startling moment where, I believe, a Christian starts and ends.

The Mary of Easter is the Easter of Mary on your face and mine. Many canvases later, she is still the face I'll recognize with eyes closed.

In time, much time, I began to see others. If Lydia, Phoebe or Priscilla once lurked in the Latin, they seldom came through. Sarah stayed in her tent with an unholy laugh. Eve hid the face that was covered with sin; Hagar was lost in the wilderness. Martha drowned under pots and pans, and sister Mary just kept quiet. Others never had a name. The Spirit of Wisdom, who could not be contained, was obscure in lofty clouds.

I stuck to the work of re-membering through the tenacity of a man — my husband, Gene. Our sharing, especially his hard edge question, "What's really going on here?" — asked over and harder — helped me to allow each canvas, each new presence, to reveal hope and possibility.

We're both glad to be living in this evolving, evocative moment of the Spirit.

May Mary of Nazareth laugh from your canvas
and may that laughter of Wisdom
spill over infectiously
into the vale of tears.

In your story of living,
may you feel the caress of a hand,
and the wonder of your own.

You are here. You write and paint.

13

Eve is the final touch from the hand of the Potter whose fingerprints were impressed on her forever.

Eve

(Genesis 1—3)

Eve comes alive, dripping wet, from God's fingers,
capstone of Creation in clay.
Unique,
herself.
She was the final touch from the hand of the Potter,
whose fingerprints were impressed on her forever.

Her name means "To Live."
Her face reflects what she sees in "I Am."
The Creator breathed her creative,
and there was mutual delight.
Life dawned on Eve:
It was hers to be lived.

Her first moment with God was total communion
of the poem and the Poet.
Eve's creation is full authentication
of the feminine in God.

She was wholly beautiful. She knew it.
She touched her body as God had touched it.

Hers is God-given self-image.
Eve, in this moment, is a woman without baggage.

And we are wistful.
The memory of that Original Moment
is buried alive in the depths of us all,
beneath our baggage —
and a broken mirror.

It makes us gasp to behold something beautiful,
to grasp a moment closely.
We wonder and warm to goodness
because the Feel is still fresh —
God never washed the clay from that hand.

When Eve's eyes met Adam's,
love took to "other"
in mutual bonding.
Adam, too, had no baggage.
God had let go:
charged them with life
with all its potential.
Fully human relationship
marked the first meeting of the first human couple.

It was wholesome.
In communion with each other,
each was sexuality without shame.
The goodness in pleasure

and the pleasure in goodness
were warped in the Fall,
when intimacy was broken.

In the rupture of body, mind and spirit,
body was cast as Weakness of Flesh.
Because somebody was to blame,
"body" became the generic name for "woman's sin" —
Eve's.

And Adam was afflicted with a dominance disorder.

God had potted the apple
that hung in the background.
Sin was in the bites
of two sets of teeth.
The apple grew on the Tree of Knowledge
tended by God
near the Tree of Life.

God knows
there is none of that apple in pie in the sky.
When Eve ate of the fruit,
she laid hold of the real world . . .
where there came the Tree of Jesus
for ever-new creation.

There came an Easter Exultet,
singing of "the happy fault" that brought him here.
Jesus enables the living

continually
to bring forth his Spirit in the world.

New Creation is such an incredibly good idea
it had to be God's.

New Creation is charged
with the sacred capacity for life
in an earthen vessel.
The body of Christ that saved us.
The body of Christ that is Eucharist.
The body of Christ that is church
as we are.

Body is a healing place
where person comes together;
a good place to be,
to interact,
to be of some earthly good.
It will be raised up to live in forever.

New Creation, always wet and expansive,
exposes distortions and half-truths
misshaping
this earthside and beautiful body of Christ.
Our faces bring out radiance
in the faces of God.

Woman looks back to step forward.
She was the final touch in creation made whole.
And the Father danced.

Sarah is a clock that God forgot to wind who suddenly began to chime.

Sarah

(Genesis 17:15-22; 18; 21:1-7)

Laughter is at the genesis of salvation history,
in a child named Laughter.

Sarah is a clock that God forgot to wind
who suddenly began to chime.

Sarah's watch is upon us,
and take it from mother,
so is her Laugh.

Her God of the Unexpected
makes full bloom in the ice of January,
spring in winter on an almond tree.
Jeremiah calls the almond tree,
with its crown of white,
a sign of the glory of old age.
It was "the prophet's tree,"

21

one who waits for God's word to be fulfilled.
Did Sarah count numbers
under a canopy of blossoms?

She had waited and waited.
She is seasoned survivor.
The old woman incarnates the weakness
and strength
of faith grown knotted and gnarled,
the "and yets" and "not yets" of hope
wilted and worn.
She's the failure inherent in faithfulness.
In her own body, she is age that is past
and yet pregnant with future.

At 90, Sarah sang:
"God has given me cause to laugh,
and all who hear of it will laugh with me!"

The Great Laugh of the mother of promise
is the prophetic glad moment,
a birth wail ripening over the long course
of the salvation story.
Sarah's mirth may have been
an early epiphany of Laughing God,
who has made a habit of showing up
in untimely fashion on unlikely faces.

Preparing the way for the blessed event to Abraham,
God said:
"I am El Shaddai."

(An early advent of that title of Mother God
renders it "God of the Open Wastes.")*
Abraham, caught by surprise, laughed to himself.
Enough already, he conveyed to God.
And the One who names names insisted:
"Yes, *Sarah* . . ."

Sarah's long dark journey
was not dotted with wonder
by little lights from the sky.
Night lay in watching and wanting
as her husband, chosen father,
counted descendants by numbers of stars.

God conversed with Abraham alone.
The "princess," named to be mother of kings,
chosen to partnership in risk and response,
remained sterile.

Years had left behind
a hard-nosed realist,
and yet a mettle
that wouldn't settle for the status quo.
She always persevered — if sometimes loosely.

Sarah listened.
God caught her by surprise behind a tent,
when she was well past surprising.

---

* Cf. *The New Jerusalem Bible*, Gn 17, footnote b.

23

Life had proceeded to paint her
into a corner
and nearly succeeded, for she had acceded.
Such was the wasteland
opened by El Shaddai.

Sarah's large moment began at her smallest.
She let go and let God —
emptied of a lurking smirk
that grace replaced with a full belly-laugh.

Sarah cooperated with pleasure.
Afraid to believe, she did anyway.
Beyond bells, she chimed.

Now, she twinkles from heaven
in those who say thank you to God
at the most impossible moments.
In her memory, recall them.

She developed an acute sense of timing.
Attuned to our moment,
Sarah's a person who has stopped playing dead.

There is movement in Sarah.
She's a sign of the time
not to waste.
Her faithfulness moves mountains
by climbing them.

Time for grown-up children of the "mother of nations"
— especially daughters —
to reach high for her blossom being blown in the Wind
and bring it down to earth.
Then shake the tree.

Sarah's laughs
are for those who hold on
yet get out of the way,
giving up only to God,
who is ever Surprise.

Laughter will be born free again. Take it from Sarah.
This watch,
it's a girl!

Hagar's wilderness cried of the absence and presence of God.

Hagar

(Genesis 16; 17:20; 21:8-21)

There's a song of the desert
reserved for romantics.
It is not in Hagar's range.

Her wilderness cried
of the Absence and Presence of God.
Good God! Where are You?
Is the sound familiar?

Some chaos is creative.
Life paints deserts on each person's space;
each has the talent and freedom
to add not a few.

Some are deep, private voids
that only God and time can fill.
We can choose to remain empty.
Hagar couldn't.

There is a spirituality of the desert
where sinner-saints thrive
in self-purging aloneness . . .
to open, expand,
and mystically drink of pure healing wells.
It is freely chosen abandonment to God.
Hagar did not run there.

There is pure devastation of spirit
in deserts of degradation,
overcrowded with outcasts
under codes of our time.
These unholy sanctuaries,
painted day after day on newsprint and tape,
are no preferential option.
Violated by hunger and thirst in a most personal way,
thousands cry out for a lifetime to God
who doesn't often appear.
Many Hagars are lost there.

"I have heard you," God said
to a runaway slave,
a victim abused for taunting her mistress.
Under the code of her times,
Hagar was "given" to Abraham by Sarah.
Hagar's consent was not required.

By a spring in the desert,
God found a daughter —
desperate and driven.
There Hagar saw, heard, and named

"God of Vision."
And there God named her unborn child, "Ishmael,"
which means "I have heard you."

Because she hearkened to God,
Hagar's name and her story
were not lost in the sands of history.
Because she went back,
an alien's child came to be,
entitled "Son of Abraham."

God spoke again in the wilderness
to the now-banished mother and son.
Their loaf was gone,
their jug was dry.
A bewildered Hagar,
too depressed to watch her son die,
hear him cry,
heard God of Vision say:
    "What is the matter, Hagar?
    Do not be afraid.
    Arise! Lift up the boy and hold him by the hand;
    for I will make of him a great nation."
And again God manifested Presence
with drinking water.

This time, Hagar was not asked to return.
God was with them
"as the boy grew up in the wilderness."
There
hovered the great Mother Bird of desert high places.

29

In such space the psalmist cried,
"Be not afraid . . .
I will raise you up on eagle's wings."

The grandmother of the Arab nation struggled on,
staking her family claim,
as her son married an Egyptian.

It is God who cries out in the wilderness today:
God-with-us is homeless,
> landless,
> penniless,
> powerless,
> faceless,
> voiceless,
> Hagar and her child.

Conversely,
it is we-with-God who manifest Presence,
under the guise of water and bread.

Who would perceive God
in such incredible absence?

Where is the Vision?

Many call; so few seem chosen.
"I have heard you."
We move from abandonment in God
to the abandoned of God.

Elizabeth's gladness at the sight of Mary took a quantum leap as John recognized Jesus.

Elizabeth and Mary

(Luke 1)

As Mary approached,
Elizabeth *knew*.
"Who am I
that the mother of my Lord should visit me?"

Fiery sky, hills rosy with glory,
barren trees bowing to the Wind . . .
nature reflects the passage of the Spirit
in a meeting place.
Two hands joined in a rite,
the Old Testament yielding its life to the New.

In loneliness and lowliness,
each woman arrived
to believe in the other.

Elizabeth was a background person
called forth by "*my* Lord"
and a cousin.

Her gladness at the sight of Mary
took a Quantum Leap
as John recognized Jesus.
In body language of the Spirit,
greetings bounced from unborn to Unborn.

Pious legend holds that Mary,
keeping her Secret to herself,
took to the hills
to assist her old cousin,
then six months along.

Magnanimity
occasioned the Magnificat.
And more.

An unwed pregnant teenager
welcomed the warm space
of wise old human hugging
before facing the future
Out There.
To let just the present
slowly sink in.

The three months together
was a time to tell stories,
big and little stories that connected their lives.
These are the her-stories
that nobody knows.

In the days between the old and the new,
each became her sister's keeper.

Tears and fears
were as safe between Elizabeth and Mary
as awesome joy.
Each surely needed to let herself go.
The two grew as friends,
working and praying and resting in God.

As she came out of hiding,
Elizabeth left behind
blame and embarrassment,
fear of gossip,
and little-old-ladyness.
She threw off her cape in the Spring,
and wind has a way with a veil.

Meanwhile,
where was the priest Zachariah?
Probably around the house,
where he found a retreat
away from the incense.

Unable to talk,
and possibly to hear,
he watched —
meeting himself
and the Priest Forever
there in the stillness
with Mary and Elizabeth.

Joseph?
Out There, he lay Dreaming.
Wisdom saw to that.

Graced by God and each other,
two women came to the fuller dimensions
destined for them.

"His name is John."
The mother spoke up
in an astonished assembly
to name him.
The father wrote on a slate,
standing behind her.
Zachariah received his own jolt of the Spirit
when, then,
his tongue broke loose
in prophecy and praise.

The other child was born,
called Emmanuel, God-with-us.
Elizabeth prepared the way.
They had met.

Mary of Bethany broke free to waste time with God.

Mary of Bethany

(Luke 10:38-42)

We live stressed and pressed. Preoccupied.
Oh, to be a Mary!

Mary of Bethany took her place sitting down
as foresister of all who listen, learn, reflect
on Jesus and his gospel.

She broke free
to waste time with God.

Mary was a quiet young woman
leading an orderly little life in the pattern of the times.
An intense interior nature
surfaced only in her eyes;
and no one sought to find out
what her thoughts were about.

She was sensitive and sensible,
sifting and sweeping her hours away.

Her days were ordered by her take-charge sister Martha,
and the house of the man, brother Lazarus.
Surrendered to solicitude,
she was Kept Busy.

Within narrow walls that enclosed her,
little sister saw a lopsided world
from a safe hiding place.
If she felt boxed in or bored,
she was too pious to show it.

But hospitality was a code the household practiced
religiously,
and the door was open.
One day Jesus walked in.

Mary's eyes never left him.
Her feet barely budged.
Her ears never heard her sister,
calling from the cupboard.
Hers was pure contemplation.

Mary broke rank
to sit at the feet of the Guest
and listen to him . . .
to learn from the Rabbi.
It was not the pattern for women.
Jesus not only encouraged her to stay,
but also told Martha, gently but firmly,
she worried too much.

Mary sat there,
conversant with Truth,

taking in
every word of the Word.

Whatever Jesus said
was written on her heart.
She knew her future would change
in the range of the Light
that came in and led out.
Indeed, Jesus came back to Mary
and she did to him.

When he said,
"Mary has chosen the better part,
and it will not be taken from her,"
Jesus underwrote
a free decision.

It enabled Mary to come off the sidelines
and take a new place beside him.
Jesus never told her what she had to do.
He just broke a pattern.

And he who always graced the table,
shifted the base of hospitality
to one person's space for another
as he sat there with Mary . . .
at a Reception.

Contemplation is a hard choice
for the duty-bound,
the discipline-free,

and for all of us who know
our time and space so well.

Contemplation dislodges.
It moves from heart to head to feet,
and loves reversing order.
Always expansive,
it learns to laugh and cry with a Friend
just in breaking up boxes.
Life can be spent
in a lopsided carton
labeled "Mechanics of Living."
Contemplation relocates.
It even lets God come out of a box.

We face unmarked paths and heights and crossroads,
and must contemplate unknowns.
We cling to the familiar
while it slips away underfoot.
Caught up in time,
we worry much.

Mary chose . . . to listen to him.
It's still the first choice.

Centering on Jesus
gives and takes Artistic Liberty.

What better part will not be taken away?
The answer is discovered
between two persons —
one of them is Jesus.

A Woman at a Well became a first evangelist through a capacity for belief she could not contain.

A Woman at a Well

(John 4:1-42)

An enduring, endearing feature
of an anonymous woman
was that she didn't apologize for herself.

Jesus, tired from a long, hot journey,
sat down alone by a well.
A woman with a jar came by to draw water.
"Give me a drink," he opened, that simply.

He surprised her by speaking,
and she was just as direct:
"How is it you ask me for something to drink?"
When silence was golden,
these were no standard lines.
Among his countrymen who bypassed the region,
water in the jar of a Samaritan woman
was considered impure.

45

Her eyes were not downcast,
her look asked, "Who *are* you anyway?"
It is an ongoing personal question.
Pivotal.
Pursuant to relationship,
it breaks through stiff or safe or shallow
communication.

Jesus, the Outsider,
was the first among equals
to evangelize an outsider, a woman.
One without identity
was among the first persons he told who he was,
in one of his longest conversations
with anyone in the gospels.
The Man-without-a-bucket
offered her Living Water.

Amazement fastened her eyes on him.
A skeptic well-acquainted with ways of religion,
she evaded his offer at first.
Warily and wearily,
she brought her real everyday earthy water.
And she stayed with the dialogue,
even pushed it along.

Then he spoke the truth about her lifestyle
and neither turned away.

It was a Turning Point.
She talked, at the juncture, of sacred places.
He went beyond, to spirit and truth,

46

and struck at her core.
"I know the Messiah is coming," she ventured.

The woman herself is the earthen vessel
over whom Jesus, the Word of God, replied:
"I who speak to you am he."

It was a Consecrating word.
Scripture's Sword of the Spirit
penetrated the darkness where she beheld herself.
A groundswell
broke through the mortar that held her unclean.

How much welled up inside her!
Unworthiness was placed in his hand
as an offering of gift.
She traded it in, and he drank it all in.
Living Water in return
was perhaps the first water
she had ever been given.

Entrusted, she was trustworthy.
And from where she stood,
displaced,
the greater risk was hers.

She left the water jar . . . drawn up.
She ran off to bring back a town.
Jesus needed that groundswell.
It was pure and extraordinary refreshment.

Unique to this story of a woman with shadows,
repentance is not the theme.
She became a first evangelist
through a capacity for belief she could not contain.

But then,
did Jesus ever meet a woman
whom he chided for unbelief?

Weariness had been plunged into the Old Well
every day,
almost as long as salvation itself.

Anonymity identifies all of us
who are tired from the journey.

> There's a well
> at a juncture
> where there's Jesus.
> "Who *are* you anyway?"
> "Who are *you* anyway?"
> "Give me a drink."

"Daughter of Abraham," Jesus named her, claimed her . . .

A Stooped Woman

(Luke 13:10-17)

Healing is in process.

She is empowered
to stand straight and free.
A small, bony woman
bent over double with her eyes to the ground,
had shuffled around
the house of worship for years.

Lost in her drab grayness
amid the richness of the surroundings,
she was concealed behind a golden screen
in "women's place."

Jesus came to teach one day
and lines were crossed.
He went behind bars
or she boldly bypassed them.

51

When he saw the double outcast,
Jesus called her to him.
That was her first Surprise.
She had the backbone to come
as fast as she could.

"Woman,
you are freed of your disability!"
Jesus laid hands
on one who was shunned;
touch was Startling.
It sped through her vertically,
and she glorified God
while stretching her back.

There was exclaiming!
In front of the whole assembly,
its leader, incensed,
put the Healer on the carpet.
He shook a fist and pointed a finger
at the Sign of Contradiction —
setting a captive free on the Lord's day!

"Hypocrite!" Jesus shamed him.
"Daughter of Abraham," Jesus named her,
claimed her,
perhaps the first time
such title was conferred.

Did she keep her stature in the family
when it gathered again?

A question mark—?—
is the shape of sexism
on the back of society today.
The answer,
an exclamation point—!—
is making its way . . .

Both are body-signs of church
called to repentance and healing
even on Sunday.

Ever since Jesus,
woman has been backbone of church.
Shortly thereafter,
she was returned to the background.

She has always been where church is,
her head bowed not only in prayer.
Schooled in retreat,
she was put on a pedestal
where movement is strictly limited.
She was cautiously raised to the altars;
they are women's reserve
for virgins and martyrs.

"God's Will" resigned her,
designed and assigned her
Blessed Endurance
with assurance.

Her given virtue was not to complain,
nor seek to attain.

53

With true humility,
it is hers to renounce.

Out of experience and prayer,
she's talking back and walking ahead.
She is beyond the reach
of a pat on the head.
It deprives her; circumscribes her.
Exclusion disables; inclusion enables.
Behind the screen of golden rhetoric,
who knows better? It is *her* back!

She's a Crossing Point,
a shunned world
the church fears to touch
for fear it will touch back.
It will.

Raised by Jesus
to a lonely vantage point
in an obscure house of worship
in an unnamed town,
an anonymous woman
is a sign of Good News!

Hers is a very little story,
seldom told on Sunday.

We are witnessing a new miracle
of empowering one another.
We glorify God
in stretching our backs!

Martha breaks her own stereotype; the lesser soul in its lower sphere of the workaday world.

Martha

(John 11:1-44)

The rocky tomb showed starkly
near a grove of olive trees
in a village on the road to Jerusalem.

Where was Jesus anyway? Martha had worried.
He was late. Very late.
Her lasting legacy begins "Even now."

She slipped out of the house
of mourners
with a jug of water for the Traveler.

"Lord, if you had been here,
my brother would not have died,"
she greeted him, then added,
"Even now,
I know that God will grant whatever you ask."

57

Amid bare desolation,
blazing skies herald the encounter
between Jesus and Martha
that opened the way for God's glory to be revealed.

The Word's self-revelation
as Resurrection and Life
was made in this private moment
with just a Martha.

Forthcoming and forthright,
she arrived Overshadowed
at her own moment of truth.

"I have come to believe you are the Messiah,"
she assented.
Martha's spontaneous profession of faith,
perhaps the strongest in the gospels,
may have surprised her.

She sealed her faith and her future
in the Life who came Late
even then and there.
Emerging from the meeting
on the outskirts of town and time
was a person who learned, by heart,
what it is to believe.

She had known the Friend would come.
She expected: Him.

Was Martha the picture of expectant faith?
"Lord, it's been four days. He'll be stinking,"
she said,
when the Resurrection ordered the stone rolled away.

She exemplified vulnerability —
the vitality of spirituality,
stripped to bare bones.

Martha showed the workings of faith
not so much by believing in miracles
but by sticking her neck out.
Maybe she'd begun to have it both ways.
Maybe.

The assertiveness of Martha
was home-grown.
She was never passive.
She leaped
and she led.
She was first in the house
to wake up in the morning
just to get a headstart on each day.

But her house was so open to the Spirit
that Jesus could be fully human,
fully God,
at the grave of a brother.

Martha breaks down her own stereotype:
the lesser soul

in its lower sphere
of the workaday world.
If there lived a saintly symbol somewhere
of lesser virtue,
little influence,
limited resources,
the name wasn't Martha.

She combines activism and access to God,
using her initiative
to bring them together.

Single-mindedness
crowded out all that worry about many things.
Her courage of conviction is commonly called
spunk.

God cried and laughed and ate very late
in the village of Bethany
on the slopes of the Mount of Olives
along the road to Jerusalem.

The hearty faith
of the Martha he dined with
discloses stable Vital Signs.
Even now.
Especially now.

And in a moving moment crowned with compassion, Jesus was glorified in eyes that received him.

A Woman Anointing Jesus

(Matthew 26:6-13; Mark 14:3-9)

As the End of the Week was closing in,
"a woman" burst onto the scene
and broke the heavy air
with an alabaster jar.

An unknown intruder arriving during dinner
to minister to One of the guests.
Perhaps the day before his arrest and crucifixion,
anointing his head
with rich perfumed oil.

The room that it filled
must have stilled to a collective gasp.
The men reclining at dining
could, if they would,
interpret such a gesture.
A standing prophet in Old Testament tradition
thus recognized a king, prophet, or priest . . .
one chosen by God for a sacred task
about to commence.

63

Her very presence confronted,
affronted table manners.
The overture observed more than omissions
of a half-hearted host.

A moment took pause
before his hour began . . .

It was Mission she ordained.
A face and an arm poured forth silent Amen;
a hesitant hand would be laid to touch him.
Amid rising protest,
Jesus fully accepted her ministry.

"Wherever the gospel is preached
in the whole world,
what she has done will be told
in memory of her,"
declared Jesus, the Christ.

And Understanding
beheld in a glance
— in an anointed tear for the Anointed One —
the sacred sense of Knowing.

Jesus saw *her*: a prophet.
"By perfuming my body,
she is anticipating
its preparation for burial."

She saw *him*, Lamb of God.
king, prophet, priest . . . wholly One.

Others who had hoped in him
had not expected the unkingly cross.

This is Prelude.
Like foretasting the Last Supper,
a last one stole in first
to the table of the Lord,
and perceived the substance
of Consecration.
Before the night he washed the disciples' feet,
his were bathed with her tears.
He was given a sacrament of presence
by a person he may never have met.

And in a Moving Moment crowned with compassion,
Jesus was glorified
in eyes that received him.

Did she disappear
just as quickly as she came?
Scripture carries no certain trace.
Only her memory is telling.

At a crossroad,
"a woman" risked a leap of faith
that was not really blind
because she believed the Messiah was there.
Ministry to him
caused her to be
a broken alabaster jar.
Her tear, the cost of caring,
is perfume stored in the flask of God.

65

"What she has done"
invites us all in
to reflect the cross in the eyes of another,
to discern those peculiar moments
when the pull and the pain
of particular persons
are nearer or clearer
than the Poor-always-with-us.

What is told for all time
is that Presence to Another
defines the heart of ministry,
whatever its name.

Her story, told in art,
has long overlooked
the anointing . . .
of the Head awaiting its Crowning with thorns.

She invites us to wonder.
To pause, look again.
It's *our* moment intruding.

The oils in a lamp
glow like paint of the Spirit —
garbing it red
in memory of her.

Easter took over her face like a mask. The moment is revelation now and forever.

Mary of Magdala, I

(John 20:11-18; Mark 16:9-11)

Be still and know that I am God.
The Creator smiled, as earth under stress
stirred in its sleep.

Something wonderful happened in the dark
that nobody saw
or heard.
With nary a wail,
Life Came as never before.

The silent holy night
held its ground
until the Vine that was Cut
stood,
perceived as a gardener,
and broke the first words of Easter:
"Woman, why are you weeping?
Who are you looking for?"

Mary Turned,
and a whole world would turn with her.

Two words, "Mary!" "Rabboni!"
and Easter took over her face like a mask.
The moment is Revelation
now and forever.

Rising up from her darkness of fear and sadness,
Mary pulled to her feet
with hands on his Rock,
called from long lonely vigil
at the place where they laid him.

In that private moment,
crocuses clustered at Mary's feet.
Where flowers had dried among the rocks,
earth previewed in color
the Eternal Moment
when all tears are dried.

When only emptiness filled her world,
an artist with fingers as numb as her heart
was drawn to the life
on the void of a canvas.
Drawing a blank again and again,
she squinted and squirmed, squandered the time.
But yearning was learning —
and Turning.
Inspiration came, an ecstatic moment,
and she wanted to clutch it

lest it slip from her hand.
Somehow it did:
A bright spot of color dripped on the canvas
and dropped to the ground.

And only the Creator,
who stirred paint through the night,
saw Wisdom on her morning round
tipping the can.

"That doesn't look like a flower," Mary was told.
Commissioned by Jesus to spread the Good News,
the apostle to the apostles
was not believed.

Would Jesus elect a *woman*
chosen friend and confidante?

Plausibility became no problem
later on . . . and on . . .
as her-story was developed.
The classic penitent stereotype of Mary
overtook Easter's apostle by leaps and bounds,
though evidence of a faded, jaded beauty —
not too repentant —
lies only in art and legend.
Her restoration is proceeding.

Those "seven demons expelled"
still send hell's bells aringing,
too often heard as sex as in sin.

But scriptural language described in its way
the immensity and intensity of affliction
and the depth of Mary's healing
at the hand of Jesus.

The transformation of person,
from a Calvary of mental or physical illness or both,
to wholeness,
was a resurrection of its own.

Societal stigma
lost its trace on her face
at Easter's first call.

The evident Good News Easter's Mary proclaims
is not an empty tomb
but her own experience
of *our* Crocus God.

Her story continues.
The words that broke night in the garden of Easter
speak privately to each of us.

This is Easter morning,
from a woman's point of view.

The apostle is a woman. Alleluia!

Mary advanced in the experience of age and the aging of experience.

Mary of Nazareth

(Acts 1:12-14; 2:1-4)

It took almost fifty years
and one very Windy day
for all those tears to break out on her face
in laughter.
The overshadowing of the Spirit
dissolved in Burning Light
as Wisdom came to rest on the Mother of Jesus
at Pentecost.

Amid tongues, she was speechless
with Understanding.
Comprehension.
Pain making sense.
Stored-up mystery was released in radiance;
and Mary was so happy she cried.

Pentecost reveals on a face transparent
a chosen one's choices —
the inclusiveness, conclusiveness

of many a yes
to a purity purged of anything less.
Perhaps for Mary,
Pentecost was Easter.

For the only person in the gospels
to be with Jesus throughout his life on earth,
the Spirit came full circle in joy,
on a long, winding way.

The integrity of person that developed
is cause to ponder purity
far larger than chastity,
a maturity
unknown to her glorified "yes."
It moves from the girl
graced beyond comprehension.
She is no longer all white and blue and gold,
and did not walk to Pentecost in a May procession.

Mary's maturing was not supernatural.
Yes did not happen Once and For All.

She struggled through,
muddled too.
In her years of prayerful pondering,
grace was building on nature
that had growing pains.
Yes was successive, progressive.
Mary advanced in the experience of age
and the aging of experience.

In daily deliberation,
she hand-carried grace

to its laughter in Wisdom.
Grace was full-blown
when its freshness was memory;
its largesse
was as large as life fully lived.

In youth,
Mary allowed God to make something beautiful,
and an angel confided
that *she* was to do it.
In her maturity,
the Wisdom of Jesus conveyed to his mother,
"I told you so."

The letting go that began
when Mary-with-Child
braved institutionalized negation
reached Pentecost
in face-to-face reconciliation
with friends who deserted her Son.

At its onset of labor contractions
in an upper room,
the Infant Institution experienced as one
the breath and the breadth of Confirmation.

Then Mary let go again.
Old age followed
in the way of old age:
uneventfully.
Her hair got grayer and her face more deeply lined.
The eyes which absorbed such pain and gladness

bore witness to that intensity
the rest of her days.

Ever after Pentecost,
there was a sacred place of emptiness
without husband or Son
that no church could fill,
and Wisdom never denied her.

Some of us know:
Time has a way of getting on.

We learn to live fully
more in questions
than answers.
In our own journey of faith
from Christmas
to Easter
to Pentecost —
and between and beyond —
Mary's years
are the Holy Probe for meaning.
From abnegation to affirmation: Integration.
Realization.

The Word is made flesh
and dwells among us.
Mary's wisdom is near
    whenever, however, whoever
shows God-with-us . . . here.

Grace and gladness will not be wanting.

Priscilla sought and brought out the giftedness in others.

Priscilla

(Acts 18; Romans 16:3-5; 1 Corinthians 16:19; 2 Timothy 4:19)

Priscilla was there
in a time of Transition,
radiating the new Presence of Jesus
through the living Word.
She was a first generation woman of church
whose teaching and preaching gifts
were generated by way of Pentecost.

It was a time of hindsight and foresight.
The city of God was borne earthside
in a Whirlwind of Gifts.
Unwrapped.
They were needed and heeded.
Signs of their veilings blown off
spread with the gospel.
Church had the insight
to recognize and exercise the fact
that some women were more gifted than some men.

One was Priscilla.
She marked new Common Cause:
Her gifts were unencumbered by gender.

The roving Good News drew on her skills,
developed by living,
in the art of communication.
She understood education
because Understanding had grasped her:
taught what it is
to bring forth to light.
Inspired preaching, in wisdom and knowledge,
warmed very early
to that sense of the Spirit.

"Not only I but all the Gentile churches
are grateful to Prisca and Aquila,"
writes Paul to the Romans.
The missionary pair risked their lives
as they broke holy ground.
A married couple, Christian Jews,
they were mentioned several times in *Letters* and *Acts*,
usually Priscilla first.

She dwelt in transitions.
When she spoke of Jesus unveiling the glory of God
that once had shone briefly on Moses' face,
she was informed, incisive, involved.
Centering on Jesus,
she enlarged the circle of teachers and preachers.
She sought out and brought out
giftedness in others.

That she taught the eloquent Apollos,
who was learned in scripture
but not advanced in the Way,
indicates the renown of Priscilla.

The story of Priscilla and Aquila
is an exodus of its own.
Displaced persons,
they were evicted from Rome because they were Jews.
Their ship of life was hardship;
it came early.
They learned to travel light
and watch out for each other.
The watchword that came home, likely to a tent,
was co-responsibility.

The sea is a symbol of journey together,
and later with Paul.
Co-workers the three,
even making tents.

> They cut, in the raw material,
> contours of collegiality.
> There was time to reflect
> in the wide open air,
> making a living,
> pondering all that had happened
> on the way to church.
> Did Paul learn to listen
> as hands stretched the canvas?

Church lived on-the-move with Priscilla and Aquila.
Under an Old Testament sign
of God's dwelling place,
the Good News kept unfolding.

The veil stands lifted by the Wood of a Tree.
Priscilla's charism emerged in the Breeze.

It stirred.
It was translucent.
Who has not felt it somehow, somewhere?
A new generation of Pentecost —
a sense of the right gifts at the right time —
is stirring again.

Church is a Gifted People.
She is young: Dreams are possible.
In the most mobile Spirit,
she is ever in Transition.

More than surviving,
she is always arriving.

Thanks, Prisca. And Aquila.

The deacon has a dignity about her. A confident composure. Competence.

Phoebe

(Romans 16:1-2; Ephesians 2:9, 19-22; Acts 15:41; 18:18-23)

The deacon has a dignity about her.
A confident composure.
Competence.

She fully embraced the truth of herself,
and knew her abilities.
She chose to be chosen.

Phoebe was a builder of missionary church,
whose edifice was Community.
The New Commandment to love one another
breathed at her core.
The grace on her face
was apparent and real.

Taking responsibility
was her response to the gospel.
As a deacon, she led
as in serving.

87

Hers was a non-gender ministry,
and Phoebe probably never heard herself addressed "deaconess."

Taking office,
she took care as characteristic.
It caused her to minister,
rather than to *ad*minister.
Though both verbs derive from the same root
of "service,"
one soon carried the tone of creeping over the top.

Her recognized commitment
was reflected, revered.
In a unique letter of recommendation
to a Roman community,
Paul calls Phoebe
deacon, sister, and patron.
She was established as a deacon at Cenchreae
before Paul's endorsement.

A prominent, influential
woman of means,
Phoebe expended herself expansively,
enabling others.
She did not keep church as a museum piece.

When she traveled,
she was always pointed
to the new Temple of the Spirit.

House churches are where
the missionary communities happened,
and Phoebe was there
at her door.
She lived for a while among the Ephesians,
where Paul carved the imagery
of "living stones."

It is apt. It befits the ways of Phoebe.

> To make something new,
> there once was a time
> to gather stones.
> It came upon a place
> on a Cornerstone,
> in a circle of sisters and brothers
> under open skies
> of an inner courtyard
> of a home,
> where the very stones cried out
> the New Temple.
> Thereupon,
> an artisan preached of pebbles,
> "Church,
> we are God's work of art!"

Phoebe's sandals knew many a stone
as they carried Good News
over mountains and valleys.

As patron,
she was resource and advocate.
As sister,
she patronized no one.
Beyond her doors she opened others,
making her voice heard for the voiceless
in church and society.

Justice tended those classic concerns
always akin
to basic human rights.
She may have changed a few structures.

An edifice of Phoebe's kind
will never be an archeological find.
It is ever and only
a joining of people.

When she began all over again,
Paul asked of church
a worthy welcome,
and "help with whatever she needs from you;
as she herself has come to the help of many —
including myself."

His words reverberate.

Where it is an honor to serve,
honor is rightly bestowed.
Phoebe, the deacon, is our sister too.

Lydia, in purple, served bread and wine as all shared together the intimacy of Presence.

Lydia

(Acts 16)

This is a way it might have been . . .
a story told in a primary color.

Red was the softness
that came through a window
at day's rite of passage.
Red was the time a young church gathered,
with the hostess
presiding at table.

Just to behold the Great Red of sunset
was in itself a partaking of God.
Lydia, in purple,
served bread and wine
as all shared together
the intimacy of Presence.
Red can be rapture
that erupts into song.
Red is the glory

in spontaneous silence,
hearing the heartbeat
of God-with-us within-us.

There at the table was no Jew or Greek,
none slave or free,
no woman or man.
All was one.
Lydia freely gave of a gift,
drawn forth by a family of faith.

Red was the celebration of Revelation
and the revelation of Celebration
at a feast of thanksgiving.
Of such is New Wine.

Gratitude was colored by other settings.
The Glad News had crossed a sea,
and come to Philippi
from a riverside and a jail.

> Lydia was Paul's first European convert,
> a single person who was head of a household,
> and a merchant in cloth
> dyed purple.
> She wore it well:
> a blend of the blue of wisdom
> and the red of courage.

Paul and Silas had gone outside the city gates
to find the Sabbath place of prayer.

They sat down and spoke to "the women"
who were gathered near the water.

One who listened was Lydia,
and her fervent heart was opened.
After she and her household were baptized,
she said to the homeless missioners:
"If you are convinced I believe in the Lord,
come and stay in my house."

In her "noted" persistence,
church found a lasting new base.

Color it red,
the Baptism of Fire
experienced early by church in Philippi.

    Within walls of a prison
    in the middle of the night,
    Paul and Silas, red from beating,
    sang praise,
    and lonely captives
    forsook groaning to listen.
    When a sudden Great Tremor opened all doors,
    everyone's chains fell off
    and nobody left.
    Unfettered feet likely limped into dance.
    And by dawn,
    the jolted and jubilant jailer
    was spreading a table.
    Conversions?

Whoever, trembling, gives thanks
for an earthquake,
has learned overnight
to rejoice in all things.

Paul and Silas stopped by a houseful of church
on their way out of town.
Red is the lifeblood
of joy in the Lord.
Red is release of an energy
that will not be confined.
Church in Philippi
sprang from a base —
from a family, or two,
formed by the Word.

Paul longed to come back.
His letter to the Philippians,
written in prison,
may have been read the first time
to a church gathered for supper
at Lydia's house.

It may also have gone
to a jail.

Red, the boldest of primary colors,
was made to take over.
To Philippi was given
the Epistle of Joy.

To Mary, Wisdom dispatched a flash of fruition
via daystar . . . and distance. The apostle is a woman. Alleluia.

Mary of Magdala, II

Mary of Magdala always saw Easter
from the perspective of person.
How often she must have Returned
to the Rock near the Tomb.
Just to be there. Alone.

Friday, Saturday, Sunday
reverted to Ordinary Time;
and earth resumed tilting and turning
in all shades of color
from darkness to light.

Mary absorbed that dyeing of living.
But Three Days spanned a lifetime
that was never the same.
The staying power of love
that Easter could not cling to
secured self-esteem,
recharged her commitment.

99

"Woman, why are you weeping? Who are you looking for?"
As Easter took on the new life of church,
the second Mary chosen to bear the Good News
would muse on the words . . .

Jesus had sent her
to tell what she saw and heard
in their great moment together.
Moments got small. Peter kept complaining.
She soon became *that* woman —
who sounded as if Jesus continued to confide in her.

Mary always leaned to the Rock,
and refused to crouch again in fear.

Years after Life Came in a Tomb,
we can sense Mary there,
coming to firm up her belief in herself,
to hear again the music of that call.

What might have happened,
there at the Rock?

    Nature, nudged by heaven, remembered . . .
    Earth removed holy mud from its eye,
    and vision persuaded, pervaded the night.

    To Mary,
    Wisdom dispatched
    a flash of fruition
    via daystar . . . and distance.

Summitry
tapped on a mountain's steep, rocky slopes.
A far-off sister danced among flowers,
her arms a wide Alleluia.

Instinctively, Mary lifted the hand
that held her Easter bud
to salute its Unfolding.
And in the twinkling of an eye —
a prophet's eye —
Wisdom knew that she knew.

Mary was engulfed in the nearness
of Mountain God,
Full-Breasted One,
Mother.
And the Wind carried her wakened, whispered,
"El Shaddai!"

The glimpse that was given
slipped softly away.
It was not hers
to touch or to hold;
for an instant Mary was jolted by the pang of Easter.
Again, the Turning: this time to a sister.
And the music of call
reverberated over time and space.

Apostleship
stayed on course at its Source.
She came down from the mountain humming.
For Mary, it was written on rock

that the truth of true love
was to give it away.

Her gift with people
proved a lifetime mission.
She always Returned
to the unwanted and unworthy.

A cutting edge of church,
Mary scratched the soul
of patriarchal sexism
because she knew who she was,
where she had been,
and who had her ear.

Rooted,
she routes us
to converge on the vision;
to see what might be,
not what might have been.

From her hardy First Bloom,
a flower spreads into wildflowering,
a daystar gives way to high noon.

The Edge of the Canvas
was cut early One Morning.
To behold it,
a world yearns to believe
from the perspective of person.

The apostle is a woman. Alleluia!

You gambolled all over the face of the earth, delighting with children. You who radiate rainbows, laughed.

Afterword: To Wisdom

(Proverbs 8:30-31; Wisdom 6:12-19; 7, 8)

As it is written,
I call you my sister.

Come.
You are pure and simple Wisdom,
so young and so old.
Renewing all things, you never change.

You received The Artist's commission.
You were present in God's First Word of light.

Compared to sun, moon and stars,
you take precedence.
You who designed them clearly outshine them.
Darkness never prevails over Wisdom.

You selected God's works:
all your play was creative.

105

You gambolled all over the face of the earth,
delighting with children.
You who radiate rainbows, laughed. Did you cry?
Recreate us today, so wrinkling with stress.
Confusion plays on a lack-luster world.

I am misty-eyed. Oh, how well you know mist!
I call you who calls us, all-pervading pure light.
Alight on This Moment,
wherever each of us is.
More mobile than motion,
put your shine on my shoes.

Your eyes are so keen:
your feet are so — light!

Lyrics from your Song
flow into mine . . .

Image of Goodness,
you produce prophets and friends of God.
Cause us to see them, to be them.
Insight us, incite us.
Make stars in our eyes!

    Your brilliance
    is companionship with God.
    It leads to all good things.
    Yet, as is written,
    who has understood you are mother of these?

Is friend another I,
as an ancient thinker said?

Aura of the Power of God,
imbue imagination, inspire ideals.
Emanation of Glory,
inhabit, instill.

Spotless Mirror of the Workings of God,
infiltrate the works of justice and peace.

Reflection of Eternal Light,
illume love,
in us and from us, forever — and now.

What a Spectacle you are!
Gift of God, you gift God with a prism,
suffusing, diffusing
the whole Spectrum of Color. Colors of life.
They flow and blend, help create one another.
With your vision from heights,
you perceive the harmony of the whole.
You penetrate darkness endlessly, everywhere;
dance with evening stars,
and repeatedly make mornings.

But when things are in heaven, who can search them out?

You call us to call you.
Open our eyes, widen our view!
You've been down and around — all over time.

One hand reaches out,
the other caresses the human tear,
fragile as a raindrop.
You hold it high to the cross of Jesus,
at the center of your design.

Beam us into the Word, Wisdom of Jesus —
your laser of light on the Whole Human Story.
It reaches from end to end, governing all things well.

Lead on, kindly light.
Distract, detour, detain.
Dance freely once more, tap into our lines.
Tend us your timing . . .
maybe those moments of reckless abandon.

Reach us to teach us, in the school of our lives.
Settle, unsettling, deep in our days,
deepest of all where we're set in our ways.

See the sighs that escape, those withholden within.
Whisper your secrets . . . in the groaning of pain
and the groping in dark.

Enlighten in color.
Rub us where paint is too thick or too thin.
Encircle the folly of spectator living;
encompass our gray zones.
Leave us not in the neutrals that go any which way.
Be the gray in new questions to revision our view.

And show your serenity . . . in cerulean blues;
be green as in May, keeping her cool.

    I call you, my sister. I crowd you a little.
    We, your sisters and brothers,
        watch together yet alone
        as your morning round continues.
    In *our* streets and crossroads,
        keep crying aloud, "To you . . . I call!"
    Who can resist you,
        smock smeared in all colors?

Your call is to holiness.
It's as large as the universe.
Come in here: The gate is open.